D0290140

THE FLOWERS OF EVIL & PARIS SPLEEN

SELECTED POEMS

DOVER THRIFT EDITIONS

Charles Baudelaire

Translated by
Wallace Fowlie

DOVER PUBLICATIONS, INC.
MINEOLA, NEW YORK

DOVER THRIFT EDITIONS

GENERAL EDITOR: MARY CAROLYN WALDREP
EDITOR OF THIS VOLUME: SUZANNE E. JOHNSON

Copyright

Copyright © 1963, 1964 by Bantam Books, Inc.
Copyright © Renewed 1991, 1992 by Wallace Fowlie
Copyright © 2010 by Dover Publications, Inc.
All rights reserved.

Bibliographical Note

This Dover edition, first published in 2010, contains the complete English text of *Flowers of Evil* and *Paris Spleen*, in selection, as it appeared in *Flowers of Evil and Other Works/Les Fleurs du Mal et Oeuvres Choisies: A Dual-Language Book*, by Dover Publications, Inc., in 1992.

International Standard Book Number

ISBN-13: 978-0-486-47545-5
ISBN-10: 0-486-47545-X

Manufactured in the United States by LSC Communications
47545X05   2020
www.doverpublications.com

Note

CHARLES BAUDELAIRE (1821–1867) is one of the greatest and most influential European poets of the nineteenth century. One of the things he did was to bring poetry largely out of Romanticism, in which poets commonly erected fantastic structures in the air and wove elaborate fictional narratives. Not interested in classical pomp or personal histrionics, Baudelaire composed lucidly, and with unwavering frankness, from his own (albeit sometimes hallucinatory) observations. Among prostitutes, drug dens, the suffering poor, and various other examples of Paris' moral ruin, but also in animals and children, he discovered images of the soul. These he worked into poems of brooding, desire and, at times, moving praise for the beauty he believed existed beneath the perversity and corruption of modern civilization.

Flowers of Evil (*Les Fleurs du Mal*, 1857), the work in which Baudelaire's genius is perhaps most concentrated, is a collection of poems of the greatest formal beauty and profoundest melancholy. Though this work is the result of an intensely personal mission, the exploration of pain, the poet's goal is neither to express his own unhappiness, nor to demonstrate his technical mastery, but to tear down the screens behind which our inner lives are so easily hidden, to follow his demons with true abandon, and, equally, to respond to beauty whenever blessed with a glimpse of it. Nineteenth-century France did not know quite what to make of this approach, and, on the publication of *Les Fleurs du Mal*, the author was prosecuted for obscenity and blasphemy, fined and forced to remove certain pieces from the book (restored in the key 1861 edition).

Paris Spleen (*Le Spleen de Paris*, 1869) is a poignant collection of fifty prose poems that reflects Baudelaire's pessimism towards contemporary Parisian life and his compassion for its less successful inhabitants. "Here again is the *Flowers of Evil*, but much freer, more detailed, and with more raillery," said Baudelaire as he described *Paris Spleen*. These poems, published posthumously, have become the benchmark for the development of prose poetry. *Paris Spleen* is one of the founding texts of literary modernism.

As well as a poet, Baudelaire was an important art and literary critic, and an early champion and translator of Edgar Allan Poe.

Contents

The Flowers of Evil
& Paris Spleen

THE FLOWERS OF EVIL

To the Reader

Folly, error, sin and avarice
Occupy our minds and waste our bodies,
And we feed our polite remorse
As beggars feed their lice.

Our sins are stubborn, our repentance is cowardly;
We ask high prices for our vows,
And we gaily return to the muddy road,
Believing we will wash away all our spots with vile tears.

On the pillow of evil it is Thrice-Great Satan
Who endlessly rocks our bewitched mind,
And the rich metal of our will
Is vaporized by that wise chemist.

It is the Devil who pulls the strings that move us!
In repulsive objects we find enticing lures;
Each day we go down one more step toward Hell,
Without horror, through the darkness which smells rank.

Just as a lustful pauper who kisses and bites
The martyred breast of an aged whore,
We steal, as we move along, a clandestine pleasure
Which we squeeze hard like an old orange.

Packed tight and swarming like a million maggots,
A crowd of Demons carouse in our brains,
And, when we breathe, Death into our lungs
Descends, an invisible river, with heavy wailings.

If rape, poison, the knife and arson
Have not yet woven with their pleasing patterns
The banal canvas of our pitiful fate,
It is because our soul, alas, is not bold enough.

But among the jackals, panthers, bitches,
Monkeys, scorpions, vultures, serpents,
The monsters squealing, yelling, grunting, crawling
In the infamous menagerie of our vices

There is one uglier, more wicked and more foul than all!
Although he does not make great gestures or great cries,
He would gladly make the earth a shambles
And swallow the world in a yawn;

It is boredom! his eyes weeping an involuntary tear,
He dreams of gibbets as he smokes his hookah.
You know him, reader, this delicate monster,
—Hypocrite reader—my twin—my brother!

The Blessing

When, by a decree of the sovereign powers,
The Poet comes into this bored world,
His mother, terrified and full of blasphemy,
Clenches her fists toward God, who has pity on her:

"Ah, why didn't I litter a nest of vipers,
Rather than give birth to this mockery?
A curse on that night with its fleeting pleasures
When my womb conceived my expiation!

Since you chose me from among all women
To be the disgust of my disappointed husband,
And since I cannot throw back into the fire
This weak monster, like a love letter,

I will make your hate which stifles me gush forth
On the accursed instrument of your plottings,
And I will twist this wretched tree so far
That its blighted buds will not grow!"

Thus she swallows the foam of her hate,
And, without understanding the eternal designs,
She prepares in the pit of Hell
The pyres consecrated to the crimes of a mother.

Meanwhile, under the invisible care of an Angel,
The disinherited Child is intoxicated with sunlight,
And in all he drinks and in all he eats
Discovers ambrosia and vermillion nectar.

He plays with the wind, talks with the cloud,
And singing revels in the way of the cross;
And the Spirit following him in his pilgrimage
Weeps at seeing him happy as a bird in the forest.

All those he would love look at him with fear,
Or, emboldened by his calm manner,
Vie with one another in drawing from him a complaint
And practice on him the experiments of their cruelty.

In the bread and wine destined for his mouth
They mingle ashes with filthy spittings;
Hypocritically they throw away what he touches,
And blame themselves for stepping where he stepped.

His wife cries in the public places:
"Since he finds me beautiful enough to worship,
I will take on the profession of ancient idols,
And like them I will cover my body with gold;

And I will get drunk on nard, incense, myrrh,
Genuflections, meats and wines,
To learn if I can from an admiring heart
Laughingly usurp the homage of the gods!

And, when I am bored with these impious farces,
I will lay on him my frail and strong hand;
And my nails, like the nails of harpies,
Will dig a path to his heart.

Like a very young bird trembling and palpitating
I will pull that red heart out from his breast,
And, in order to satiate my favorite beast,
Scornfully I will throw it to him on the ground!"

Toward Heaven, where his eyes see a shining throne,
The serene Poet raises his reverent arms,
And the vast visions of his lucid mind
Shut off from him the sight of cruel races:

"Be blessed, my Lord, who give suffering
As a divine remedy for our impurities
And as the best and the purest essence
Which prepares the strong for holy ecstasies!

I know that you keep a place for the Poet
In the blessed ranks of the holy legions,
And that you invite him to the eternal feast
Of Thrones, Virtues and Dominations.

I know that suffering is the one nobility
Where the earth and hell will have no effect,

And that in order to weave my mystic crown
All times and all worlds must be used.

But the lost jewels of ancient Palmyra,
The unknown metals, the pearls of the sea,
Mounted by your hand, could not suffice
For this handsome diadem shining and clear;

For it will be made only of pure light,
Drawn from the holy hearth of primal rays,
And to which mortal eyes, in their full splendor,
Are but tarnished and sad mirrors!"

The Albatross

Often, as an amusement, crewmen
Catch albatrosses, huge birds of the sea,
Who follow, indolent companions of the voyage,
The ship gliding over the salty deeps.

As soon as they have placed them on the deck,
These kings of the sky, awkward and ashamed,
Pitiably let their large white wings
Drag at their sides like oars.

This winged voyager, how gauche and weak he is!
Once so handsome, how comic and ugly he is!
One sailor irritates his beak with a pipestem,
Another mimes, as he limps, the invalid who once flew!

The Poet is like the prince of the clouds,
Who haunts the tempest and mocks the archer;
Exiled on the earth in the midst of derision,
His giant wings keep him from walking.

Elevation

Above ponds, above valleys,
Mountains, woods, clouds, seas,
Beyond the sun, beyond the ether,
Beyond the limits of the starry spheres,

My spirit, you move with agility.
And, like a good swimmer who collapses in the water,
You gaily furrow the deep expanse
With an unspeakable male delight.

Fly far away from these fetid marshes;
Purify yourself in the upper air,
And drink, like some pure divine liqueur,
The clear fire that fills the limpid spaces.

Behind the boredom and endless cares
Which burden our fogged existence with their weight,
Happy is the man who can with vigorous wing
Mount to those luminous serene fields!

The man whose thoughts, like larks,
Take liberated flight toward the morning skies
—Who hovers over life and understands without effort
The language of flowers and voiceless things!

Correspondences

Nature is a temple where living pillars
At times allow confused words to come forth;
There man passes through forests of symbols
Which observe him with familiar eyes.

Like long echoes which in a distance are mingled
In a dark and profound unison
Vast as night is and light,
Perfumes, colors and sounds answer one another.

There are perfumes as cool as the flesh of children,
Sweet as oboes, green as prairies
—And others, corrupt, rich and triumphant,
Having the expansion of infinite things,
Like amber, musk, myrrh and incense,
Which sing of the transports of the mind and the senses.

Beacons

Rubens, river of forgetfulness, garden of idleness,
Pillow of cool flesh where one cannot love,
But where life abounds and writhes ceaselessly,
Like air in the sky and the sea in the sea;

Leonardo da Vinci, deep and dark mirror,
Where charming angels, with a sweet smile
Charged with mystery, appear under the shadow
Of glaciers and pines which shut in their country;

Rembrandt, sad hospital filled with murmurings,
And decorated only with a large crucifix,
Where tearful prayers are exhaled from excrement
And abruptly crossed by a winter ray;

Michelangelo, vague place where are seen Hercules
Mingling with Christs, and rising upright
Powerful phantoms which at twilight
Rip open their shrouds when they stretch their fingers;

Anger of the wrestler, impudence of the faun,
You who collected the beauty of soldiers,
Noble heart swollen with pride, weak jaundiced man,
Puget, melancholy emperor of convicts;

Watteau, that carnival where many illustrious hearts,
Like moths, wander as flames catch them,
Fresh, light decors illuminated by chandeliers
Which pour madness over the turning dance;

Goya, nightmare filled with unknown things,
With foetuses which are cooked in the midst of a witch's feast,
Of old women at a mirror and naked girls
Adjusting their stockings to tempt the demons;

Delacroix, lake of blood haunted by evil angels,
Under the shadow of a green forest of firs,
Where, under a gloomy sky, strange fanfares
Pass, like a muffled sigh of Weber;

These curses, blasphemies, complaints,
These ecstasies, cries, tears, these *Te Deums,*
Are an echo repeated by a thousand labyrinths;
They are for the hearts of men a divine opium!

It is a cry repeated by a thousand sentinels,
An order returned by a thousand loud-speakers;
It is a beacon lighted on a thousand citadels,
A call of hunters lost in the deep woods!

For it is truth, O Lord, the best testimonial
We can give of our dignity—
This ardent sobbing which rolls from age to age
And comes to die at the edge of your eternity!

The Enemy

My youth was a dark storm,
Crossed here and there by brilliant suns;
Thunder and rain have caused such quick ravage
That there remain in my garden very few red fruits.

Now I have touched the autumn of my mind,
And I must use the spade and rakes
To assemble again the drenched lands,
Where the water digs holes as large as graves.

And who knows whether the new flowers I dream of
Will find in this soil washed like a shore
The mystic food which would create their strength?

—O grief! O grief! Time eats away life,
And the dark Enemy who gnaws the heart
Grows and thrives on the blood we lose.

Ill Luck

To raise a weight so heavy,
Sisyphus, we would need your courage!
Although we have a strong heart for the work,
Art is long and Time is short.

Far from famous graves,
Toward a lonely cemetery,
My heart, like a muffled drum,
Comes beating a funeral march.

—Many a gem lies buried
In darkness and oblivion,
Far from pickaxes and drills;

Many a flower pours forth regretfully
Its perfume sweet as a secret
In solitary shades.

Former Life

A long time I lived under vast porticoes
Which marine suns tinged with a thousand fires,
And which their tall pillars, straight and majestic,
Caused to resemble basalt caves at night.

The surge, as it rolled images of the sky,
Mingled in a solemn mystical way
The omnipotent harmonies of its rich music
With the colors of the setting sun reflected in my eyes.

It is there I lived in serene sensuousness,
In the midst of blue sky, waves, splendor
And naked slaves, impregnated with perfumes,

Who cooled my brow with palms,
And whose one care was to understand
The grievous secret which made me sad.

Man and the Sea

Free man, you will always cherish the sea!
The sea is your mirror; you contemplate your soul
In the infinite rolling of its surface,
And your spirit is not a less bitter abyss.

You take pleasure in plunging into the heart of your image;
You embrace it with your eyes and your arms, and your heart
At times forgets its own rhythm
In the noise of that wild and tameless complaint.

Both of you are dark and discreet:
Man, no one has sounded the depths of your being,
Sea, no one knows your intimate secrets,
So eager are you to retain your secrets!

And yet for countless centuries
You have fought without pity and without remorse,
So much do you love carnage and death,
O eternal fighters, O implacable brothers!

Don Juan in Hell

When Don Juan descended to the lower water
And when he had given his fee to Charon,
A solemn beggar, with eyes as proud as Antisthenes,
Seized each oar with an avenging strong arm.

Showing their drooping breasts and their opened dresses,
Some women were swaying under the black firmament,
And, like a large herd of sacrificed victims,
Trailed behind him with long moans.

Sganarelle laughing asked him for his wages,
While Don Luis with a trembling finger
Pointed out to all the dead wandering on the banks
The bold son who mocked his white brow.

Trembling under her veils, chaste and thin Elvira,
Near the perfidious husband who had been her lover,
Seemed to claim from his one last smile
Where the sweetness of his first vows would shine forth.

Upright in his armor, a tall man of stone
Stood at the helm and cleft the dark waves;
But the calm hero, leaning on his sword,
Looked at the wake and did not deign to see anything else.

Beauty

I am as beautiful, O mortals! as a dream of stone,
And my breast, on which each man is wounded in turn,
Is made to inspire in the poet a love
As eternal and mute as matter.

I preside in the heavens like a misunderstood sphinx;
I unite a heart of snow with the whiteness of swans;
I hate all movement which displaces lines,
And I never weep and I never laugh.

The poets before my great poses,
Which I seem to borrow from the proudest monuments,
Will consume their days in austere studies;

For I have, in order to fascinate these docile lovers,
Pure mirrors which make all things more beautiful:
My eyes, my large eyes with their eternal light!

The Giantess

At that time when Nature in her powerful ardor
Conceived monstrous children each day,
I would have loved living near a young giantess,
As a voluptuous cat at the feet of a queen.

I should like to have seen her body flower with her soul
And grow freely in her dreadful games;
And guess whether her heart conceals a somber flame
From the wet fog swimming in her eyes;

Feel at my leisure her magnificent shape;
Climb on the slope of her huge knees,
And at times in summer, when the unhealthy suns,

Wearying, make her stretch out across the country,
Sleep without worry in the shade of her breast,
Like a peaceful hamlet at the foot of a mountain.

The Mask

An allegorical statue in the style of the Renaissance

To Ernest Christophe, sculptor

Let us look at this treasure of Florentine grace;
In the curves of this muscular body
Elegance and Force abound, divine sisters.
This woman, a truly miraculous work,
Divinely strong, adorably thin,
Is made to preside over sumptuous beds,
And charm the idleness of a pontiff or of a prince.

—Also, see that enticing voluptuous smile
In which Fatuity parades its ecstasy;
That long sly look, languorous and mocking;
That charming face, surrounded by a veil,
In which each feature tells us with a triumphant air:
"Passion calls me and Love crowns me!"
To that being endowed with such majesty
See what exciting charm kindness gives!
Let us approach, and walk around her beauty.

Oh blasphemy of art! Oh fatal shock!
The woman with the divine body, promising happiness,
Ends at the top in a two-headed monster!

—No! this face is only a mask, a wicked ornament,
Illuminated by an exquisite grimace,
Look and see, atrociously contorted,
The real head, and the sincere face
Turned back under the shadow of the face which lies.
Poor noble beauty! the magnificent river
Of your tears ends in my anxious heart;
Your lie intoxicates me, and my soul drinks
From the waves which Grief causes to gush from your eyes!

—But why does she cry? She, a perfected beauty
Who would cast at her feet mankind conquered,
What mysterious malady eats into her supple side?
—O fool, she cries because she has lived!

And because she is living! But what she deplores
Above all, what makes her tremble to her knees,
Is that tomorrow, alas! she will have to live again!
Tomorrow, the day after tomorrow and forever—as we have to!

Hymn to Beauty

Do you come from deep heaven or do you come from hell,
O Beauty? Your eyes, infernal and divine,
Pour out both goodness and crime,
And for that you can be compared to wine.

You contain in your eyes the sunset and dawn;
You scatter perfumes like a stormy night;
Your kisses are a philtre and your mouth an amphora
Which make the hero a coward and the child courageous.

Do you come from a black abyss or do you come down from the stars?
Charmed Destiny follows your skirts like a dog;
At random you sow joy and disasters,
And you govern all and answer for nothing.

You walk over the dead, O Beauty, and mock them.
Among your jewels, Horror is not the least charming,
And Murder, among your dearest baubles,
Dances amorously on your proud body.

The dazzled moth flies to you, a candle,
Crackles, flames and says: Let us bless this torch!
The panting lover bending over his mistress
Resembles a dying man caressing his tomb.

It is of little consequence whether you come from heaven or hell,
O Beauty! huge, terrifying, artless monster!
If your eyes, your smile, your feet open for me the gate
Of an Infinity I love and have never known.

From Satan or God, what difference? Angel or Siren,
What difference, if you make—O fairy with soft eyes,
Rhythm, perfume, light, O my one queen—
The universe less hideous and time less heavy?

Her Hair

O fleece, which covers her neck like wool!
O curls! O perfume heavy with nonchalance!
Ecstasy! Tonight, in order to people this dark alcove
With the memories sleeping in this hair,
I want to shake it in the air like a handkerchief!

Languorous Asia and burning Africa,
A whole distant world, absent, almost defunct,
Lives in your depths, O aromatic forest!
As other spirits sail on music,
Mine, O my love, swims on your perfume.

I will go there where the tree and man, full of sap,
Swoon for a long time under the ardor of the climate;
Strong tresses, be the ocean swell which carries me off!
You contain, O sea of ebony, a dazzling dream
Of sails and rowers of flames and masts:

A resounding port where my soul can drink
In long draughts perfume, sound and color;
Where ships, gliding in the gold and mixed shades,
Open their vast arms to embrace the glory
Of a pure sky where eternal heat quivers.

I shall plunge my head in love with intoxication
Into that black ocean where she is enclosed;
And my subtle spirit which the rolling surface caresses
Will be able to find you again, O fertile idleness!
Infinite rockings of my embalmed leisure!

Blue hair, tent of stretched darkness,
You give me back the blue of the huge round sky;
On the downy edges of your twisted locks
My ardor grows drunk on the mingled smells
Of coconut oil, of musk and tar.

For a long time! forever! my hand in your heavy mane
Will sow rubies, pearls and sapphires,
So that you will never be deaf to my desire!
Are you not the oasis where I dream, and the gourd
From which I draw in long draughts the wine of memory?

"I Worship You"

I worship you as I worship the firmament of night,
O urn of sadness, great silent woman,
And love you, beautiful one, the more you flee from me,
And seem to me, ornament of my nights,
To accumulate ironically the leagues
Which separate my arms from the expanse of blue.

I advance to the attack, and I climb to the assault,
As a chorus of worms climb over a corpse,
And I cherish, O implacable cruel beast,
Even that coldness by which you are for me more beautiful!

A Carrion

Remember the object we saw, dear one,
    On that fine summer morning so mild:
At the turn of a path a loathsome carrion
    On a bed sown with pebbles,

Its legs in the air, like a lubricious woman,
    Burning and sweating venom,
Opened in a nonchalant cynical way
    Her body full of stench.

The sun shone on that rottenness,
    As if to roast it thoroughly,
And return a hundredfold to great Nature
    All that it joined together.

And the sky looked at the superb carcass
    Like a flower blossoming.
The smell was so strong that there on the grass
    You believed you might faint.

The flies swarmed over the putrid belly,
    From which emerged black battalions
Of maggots, which flowed like a thick liquid
    Along those human rags.

All of it descended, or rose like a wave,
    Or rushed forth buzzing;
One might have said that the body, swollen with a vague breath,
    Lived by multiplying itself.

And that world gave forth a strange music,
    Like running water and wind,
Or the grain which a winnower in rhythmic motion
    Shakes and turns in his basket.

The shapes had dimmed and were only a dream,
    A sketch slow to emerge
On the forgotten canvas, and which the artist finishes
    Only by memory.

Behind rocks a restless bitch
Watched us with angry eye,
Waiting for the moment to take from the skeleton
The piece it had relinquished.

—And yet you will be similar to that filth,
To that horrible infection,
Star of my eyes, sun of my nature,
You, my angel and my passion!

Yes! you will be like that, O queen of graces,
After the last sacraments,
When you go, under the grass and rich blossomings,
To rot among the bones.

Then, O my beauty, tell the vermin
Which will eat you with kisses,
That I have kept the form and the divine essence
Of my decomposed loves!

De Profundis Clamavi★

I implore your pity, You, the only one I love,
From the depth of the dark abyss where my heart fell.
It is a mournful universe with a leaden horizon,
Where horror and blasphemy swim in the night;

A sun without heat hovers above for six months,
And the other six months night covers the earth;
It is a country more bare than the polar land
—No beasts, no streams, no green, no woods!

For there is no horror in the world which surpasses
The cold cruelty of that icy sun
And that vast night similar to the old Chaos;

I envy the fate of the lowest animals
Who can sink into a stupid sleep,
Because the skein of time is so slow to unravel!

★The Latin title is the opening of Psalm 130: "Out of the depths have I cried unto thee."

Duellum*

Two warriors rushed at one another; their weapons
Splashed the air with streaks of light and blood.
These plays, this clinking of steel are the tumult
Of youth prey to bleating love.

The swords were broken! like our youth,
Beloved! but the teeth, the sharp nails,
Soon avenge the saber and the treacherous dagger
—O fury of matured hearts exasperated by love!

Into the ravine haunted by lynxes and leopards
Our heroes, wickedly wrestling, rolled,
And their skin will cover the arid briars with flowers.

—This abyss is hell, peopled with our friends!
Let us roll there without remorse, inhuman Amazon,
In order to make eternal the ardor of our hate!

Duellum is the archaic form of *bellem* (war), with a special connotation of two participants.

The Balcony

Mother of memories, mistress of mistresses,
You, all my pleasures! You, all my duties!
You will remember the beauty of caresses,
The sweetness of the hearth and the spell of evenings,
Mother of memories, mistress of mistresses!

Evenings lighted by the burning of the coals,
And evenings on the balcony, veiled with rosy vapors.
How soft your breast was for me! how kind your heart was!
We often said imperishable things
On evenings lighted by the burning of the coals.

How beautiful the sun is in the warm evening!
How deep is space! How powerful is the heart!
As I bent over you, queen of worshiped women,
I believed I could smell the perfume of your blood.
How beautiful the sun is in the warm evening!

Night thickened as if it were a partition,
And my eyes in the dark could hardly see your eyeballs,
And I drank your breath, O sweetness, O poison!
And your feet went to sleep in my fraternal hands.
Night thickened as if it were a partition.

I know the art of evoking minutes of happiness,
And I saw again my past hidden in your knees.
Why look for your languorous beauty
Elsewhere than in your dear body and in your gentle heart?
I know the art of evoking minutes of happiness.

Will these vows, perfumes and infinite kisses
Be born again from an abyss forbiddden to our soundings,
As rejuvenated suns climb in the heavens
After being washed at the bottom of deep seas?
—O vows! O perfumes! O infinite kisses!

"I Give You These Verses"

I give you these verses so that if my name
Happily lands in distant epochs,
And one evening makes the human spirit dream,
Vessel favored by a great northwind,

The memory of you, resembling obscure fables,
Will weary the reader like a dulcimer,
And through a brotherly and mystic link
Remain as if hanging from my lofty rhymes;

Accursed one to whom, from the deep abyss
To the highest sky, nothing gives answer, save me!
You who like a shade with tracks ephermeral,

Walk with light step and serene glance
Over the stupid mortals who have judged you badly,
Statue with eyes of jet, great angel with your brow of brass!

Semper Eadem★

You used to say, "Whence comes to you this strange sadness,
Mounting like the sea over the black bare rock?"
When our heart has once made its vintage,
To live is a curse. It is a secret known to all,

A very simple grief and not mysterious,
And, like your joy, clear to everyone.
So stop your search, O beauty so curious,
And, even if your voice is sweet, be silent!

Be silent, you who are ignorant, whose soul is always charmed,
Whose lips have a child's laugh! Much more than Life,
Death often holds us by subtle bonds.

Let, yes, let my heart grow passionate on a *lie*,
Let it sink into your lovely eyes as into a lovely dream,
And sleep for a long time under the shadow of your lashes!

★The Latin title *Semper Eadem* ("always the same") is either a feminine singular or a neuter plural.

"What Will You Say?"

What will you say this evening, poor solitary soul,
What will you say, my heart, heart once disgraced,
To that beauty who is kind and dear,
And whose divine glance has suddenly given you new life?

—We will place our pride in singing her praises:
Nothing is worth the sweetness of her authority;
The flesh of her spirit has the perfume of Angels,
And her eyes clothe us with a cloak of light.

Whether it be at night and in solitude,
Whether it be in the street and within a multitude,
Her phantom dances in the air like a torch.

Sometimes it speaks and says: "I am beautiful, and I command
That for my love you love only what is Beauty;
I am the guardian Angel, the Muse and the Madonna!"

Dawn of the Spirit

When with revelers the white crimson dawn
Comes to join the persistent Ideal,
Through the operation of an avenging mystery
An angel is awakened in the sated brute.

The inaccessible blue of Spiritual Skies,
For the crushed man who still dreams and suffers,
Opens and sinks down with the attraction of the abyss.
Thus, dear Goddess, lucid pure Being,

Over the smoky wrecks of stupid orgies
Your memory more clear, roseate, and charming,
Ceaselessly hovers before my wide-opened eyes.

The sun has darkened the flame of the candles;
Thus, always conquering, your phantom is like
The immortal sun, O soul of splendor!

Evening Harmony

Now comes the time when quivering on its stem
Each flower exhales like a censer;
Sounds and perfumes turn in the evening air;
Melancholy waltz and languorous vertigo!

Each flower exhales like a censer;
The violin sobs like an afflicted heart;
Melancholy waltz and languorous vertigo!
The sky is as sad and beautiful as a great altar of rest.

The violin sobs like an afflicted heart,
A tender heart, which hates the huge black void!
The sky is as sad and beautiful as a great altar of rest.
The sun drowned in its blood which coagulates.

A tender heart, which hates the huge black void,
Welcomes every vestige of a luminous past!
The sun drowned in its blood which coagulates . . .
Your memory shines in me like a monstrance!

An Invitation to Voyage

My child, my sister,
Think of the delight
Of going far off and living together!
Of loving peacefully,
Loving and dying
In the land that bears your resemblance!
The wet suns
Of those disheveled skies
Have for my spirit
The mysterious charm
Of your treacherous eyes
Shining through their tears.

There, all is order and beauty,
Richness, quiet and pleasure.

Highly polished furniture,
Made beautiful by time,
Would decorate our room;
The rarest flowers
Mingling their odors
With the vague fragrance of amber,
Rich ceilings,
Deep mirrors,
Eastern splendor,
Everything there would speak
In secret to the soul
Its sweet native tongue.

There, all is order and beauty,
Richness, quiet and pleasure.

Behold sleeping
On the canals those ships
Whose temperament is a wanderer's;
It is to satisfy
Your slightest desire
That they come from the ends of the world.
—The setting sun
Clothes the fields,

The canals, the entire city,
With hyacinth and gold;
The world goes to sleep
In a warm light.

There, all is order and beauty,
Richness, quiet and pleasure.

Irreparable

Can we stifle the old, the long Remorse,
      Which lives, writhes and twists,
And feeds on us as the worm feeds on the dead,
      As the maggot on the oak?
Can we stifle the implacable Remorse?

In what flask, in what wine, in what infusion,
      Shall we drown this old enemy,
Destructive and ravenous as a courtesan,
      Patient as an ant?
In what flask? in what wine? in what infusion?

Tell it, beautiful sorceress, yes, tell it, if you can,
      To this soul distraught with anguish
And like unto the dying man crushed by the wounded,
      And who is bruised by the horse's hoof.
Tell it, beautiful sorceress, yes, tell it, if you can,

To this dying man whom the wolf already detects
      And over whom the vulture is flying,
To this broken soldier! if he must despair
      Of having his cross and his tomb;
This poor dying man whom the wolf already detects!

Can one light up a murky black sky?
      Can one pierce darkness
Thicker than pitch, without morning and evening,
      Without stars, without funereal flashes?
Can one light up a murky black sky?

Hope which shines in the windows of the Inn
      Is blown out, and dead forever!
Without moon and rays, one can find where the martyrs
      Of a bad road are sheltered!
The Devil has made everything dark in the windows of the Inn!

Adorable sorceress, do you love the damned?
      Tell me, do you know what is irremissible?
Do you know Remorse, with the poisoned arrows,
      For which our heart serves as target?
Adorable sorceress, do you love the damned?

The Irreparable gnaws with its vile teeth
Our soul, that pitiful monument,
And often it attacks, like the termite,
The building at the foundation.
The Irreparable gnaws with its vile teeth!

—I have seen at times, upstage in a shoddy theater
Which a resonant orchestra enflamed,
A fairy light up in an infernal sky
A miraculous dawn;
I have seen at times upstage in a shoddy theater

A spirit, who was only light, gold and gauze,
Fling to earth an enormous Satan;
But my heart, which ecstasy never visits,
Is a theater where I wait,
Always in vain, for that Spirit with wings of gauze!

Song of Autumn

I

Soon we shall plunge into cold darkness;
Farewell, strong light of our too brief summers!
I already hear falling, with funereal thuds,
The wood resounding on the pavement of the courtyards.

All of winter will gather in my being: anger,
Hate, chills, horror, hard and forced labor,
And, like the sun in its polar hell,
My heart will be only a red icy block.

I listen shuddering to each log that falls;
The scaffold which is being built has not a hollower echo.
My mind is like the tower which falls
Under the blows of the indefatigable heavy battering ram.

It seems to me, lulled by the monotonous thuds,
That somewhere a casket is being nailed in great haste.
For whom? Yesterday it was summer; here is autumn!
This mysterious noise sounds like a departure.

II

I love the green light of your long eyes,
Sweet beauty, but everything today is bitter for me,
And nothing, neither your love, nor the boudoir, nor the hearth,
Is worth as much to me as the sun shining over the sea.

But despite all that, love me, tender heart! be maternal,
Even for an ingrate, even for a wicked man;
Lover or sister, be the passing tenderness
Of a glorious autumn or of a setting sun.

A brief task! The grave is waiting; it is avid!
My head resting on your knees, let me
Enjoy, as I grieve for the white torrid summer,
The yellow gentle ray of the earlier season!

Moesta et Errabunda★

Tell me, Agatha, does your heart, at times, fly away,
Far from the black ocean of the sordid city,
Toward another ocean where splendor breaks forth,
As blue, clear, and deep as virginity?
Tell me, Agatha, does your heart at times fly away?

The sea, the mighty sea, consoles our labor!
What demon endowed the sea, the raucous singer
Whom the huge organ of howling winds accompanies,
With this sublime function of nurse?
The sea, the mighty sea, consoles our labor!

Take me away, O train! carry me off, O ship!
Far! far! Here the mud is made from our tears!
—Is it true that at times the sad heart of Agatha
Says: Far from remorse, and crimes, and grief,
Take me away, O train, carry me off, O ship?

How far away you are, perfumed paradise,
Where under a clear blue all is love and joy,
Where all that one loves is worthy of being loved,
Where in pure sensation the heart is drowned!
How far away you are, perfumed paradise!

But the green paradise of childish loves,
Races, songs, kisses, bouquets,
Violins vibrating behind the hills,
With jars of wine, at evening, in the groves
—But the green paradise, of childish loves,

That innocent paradise, full of furtive joys,
Is it already farther away than India and China?
Can we remember with plaintive cries,
And still animate with a silver voice,
That innocent paradise full of furtive joys?

★The Latin title means "The sorrowful, wandering woman."

Cats

Fervent lovers and austere scholars
Both love, in their mature season,
The powerful gentle cats, pride of the house,
Which like them are sensitive to the cold and sedentary.

Friends of science and ecstasy,
They search for silence and the horror of darkness;
Erebus would have taken them for his funereal steeds,
If they could bend their pride to slavery.

While dreaming they take the noble attitudes
Of great Sphinxes stretched out in the heart of the desert,
Which seem to sleep in an endless revery;

Their fecund loins are full of magic sparks,
And specks of gold, like fine sand,
Add vague stars to their mystical eyeballs.

The Broken Bell

It is bitter and sweet, during winter nights,
To listen, near the fire which crackles and smokes,
To the distant memories slowly rising
At the noise of chimes singing in the fog.

Happy is the bell with the vigorous throat
Which, despite its age, alert and strong,
Faithfully sends forth its religious cry,
Like an old soldier standing sentinel under the tent!

My soul is cracked, and when in its boredom
It wishes to fill the cold air of night with its songs,
It often comes about that its weakened voice

Resembles the thick rattle of a wounded man forgotten
On the edge of a lake of blood, under a great pile of the dead,
And who dies, without moving, after tremendous efforts.

Spleen

Pluvius, irritated with the entire city,
Pours from his urn in great waves a dismal cold
Over the pale inhabitants of the neighboring cemetery
And mortality over the foggy outskirts.

My cat on the stones looking for a litter
Ceaselessly moves its thin mangy body;
The soul of an old poet wanders along the rain spout
With the sad voice of a chilblained phantom.

The bell mourns, and the smoky log
Accompanies in falsetto the wheezing clock,
While in a pack of cards full of filthy odors,

The fatal bequest of an old dropsical woman,
The handsome knave of hearts and the queen of spades
Talk darkly about their dead love.

Heautontimoroumenos*

Like a butcher I will strike you
Without anger and without hate
As Moses struck the rock!
And from your eyelid I will cause,

In order to irrigate my Sahara,
The waters of suffering to gush forth.
My desire swollen with hope
Will float on your salty tears

Like a vessel moving out from shore,
And in my heart which they will intoxicate
Your dear sobs will resound
Like a drum beating the charge!

Am I not a false chord
In the divine symphony,
Thanks to the voracious Irony
Which shakes and bites me?

The raucous girl is in my voice!
This black poison is my blood!
I am the sinister mirror
In which the megara looks at herself!

I am the wound and the blade!
I am the slap and the cheek!
I am the limbs and the wheel,
The victim and the executioner!

I am the vampire of my own heart
—One of the deserted men
Condemned to eternal laughter,
And who can no longer smile!

---

*Baudelaire probably found the (Greek) title ("The Self-Torturer") in Joseph de Maistre ("3e Entretien" of the *Soirées de Saint-Pétersbourg*); it is the title of a Latin play by Terence based on an earlier Greek play.

The Irremediable

I

An Idea, a Form, a Being
Leaving the blue and falling
Into a murky leaden Styx
Where no eye of Heaven penetrates;

An Angel, impudent traveler
Tempted by love of the deformed,
At the bottom of a huge nightmare
Floundering like a swimmer,

And struggling, O funereal anguish!
Against a gigantic whirlpool
Which sings like madmen
And pirouettes in the darkness;

A spellbound wretch
In his futile gropings,
In order to flee a serpent-filled place,
Looking for light and a key;

One damned descending without lamp,
On the edge of an abyss whose stench
Betrays the wet depths
Of endless stairways with no rail,

Where clammy monsters watch
Whose large phosphorous eyes
Create a night still blacker
And leave only themselves visible;

A ship caught at the pole,
As in a crystal trap,
Looking for the fatal aperture
Through which it fell into this jail

—Clear emblems, perfect picture
Of an irremediable fortune,
Which makes one think that the Devil
Always does well everything he does!

II

Somber clear dialogue
Of a heart which has become its own mirror!
Well of Truth, clear and black,
Where a pale star trembles,

An ironic, infernal beacon,
Torch of satanic grace,
A unique solace and glory,
—Consciousness in doing Evil!

The Swan

To Victor Hugo

I

Andromache, I think of you! This small river,
Poor sad mirror where once shone
The immense majesty of your widow's grief,
This deceptive Simoïs which grows with your tears,

Suddenly enriched my fertile memory,
As I crossed the newly built Carrousel.
Old Paris is no more (the form of a city
Changes more quickly, alas, than the heart of a man);

I see only in my mind that camp of booths,
The piles of rough-hewn capitals and shafts,
The grass, the heavy blocks turned green by the water of pools,
And, shining on the tiles, the crowded bric-à-brac.

There once a menagerie spread out;
There I saw, one morning, at the time when under a cold
Clear sky Labor awakens, when the road
Pushes a dark storm through the silent air,

A swan which had escaped from its cage,
And, with its webby feet rubbing the dry pavement,
Was dragging its white plumage over the level ground.
Near a stream without water the bird opening its beak

Nervously bathed its wings in the dust,
And said, its heart full of its beautiful native lake:
"Water, when will you rain down? When will you thunder, O lightning?"
I see that wretched bird, a strange and fatal myth,

Toward the sky at times, like the man of Ovid,
Toward the ironic and cruelly blue sky,
Stretching its avid head over its convulsed neck,
As if it were addressing reproaches to God!

II

Paris changes! But nothing in my sadness
Has moved! new palaces, scaffoldings, blocks,
Old suburbs, everything becomes an allegory for me,
And my dear memories are heavier than rocks.

In front of the Louvre an image vexes me:
I think of my great swan, with its mad gestures,
Like exiles, ridiculous and sublime,
And devoured by an unrelenting desire! And then of you,

Andromache, fallen from the arms of a great husband,
A degraded animal, in the hands of proud Pyrrhus,
Near an empty tomb bent over in ecstasy;
Widow of Hector, alas, and wife of Helenus!

I think of the Negress, thin and phthisical,
Walking in mud, and looking, with haggard eyes,
For the absent palm trees of proud Africa
Behind the huge wall of fog;

Of whoever has lost what can never
Be found again! Of those who collapse in tears
And suckle Grief as if she were a kind wolf!
Of sickly orphans drying like flowers!

As if in a forest where my mind is exiled
An old memory sounds as in a blast from a horn!
I think of sailors forgotten on an island,
Of prisoners, of conquered men! . . . And of many others!

"The Warm-Hearted Servant"

The warm-hearted servant of whom you were jealous,
And who is sleeping her sleep under humble grass,
Yes, we should take her some flowers.
The dead, the poor dead, know deep grief,
And when October, the stripper of old trees, blows
Its melancholy wind around their marble stone,
Certainly they must find the living ungrateful
In sleeping, as they do, warmly between their sheets,
While, racked by ominous dreams,
Without a bedmate, without intimate talk,
Old frozen skeletons worked over by worms,
They feel the winter snow dripping away
And the century melting, when no friends and no family
Replace the tattered wreathes hanging on the grill,

When the log whistles and sings, if in the evening
I saw her sitting calmly in the armchair,
If, in a blue cold night of December,
I found her huddled in a corner of my room,

Sedate, and coming from the depths of her eternal bed
To shield with her maternal eyes the child grown to man,
What could I answer that pious soul,
When I see tears falling from her empty eyelids?

Parisian Dream

To Constantin Guys

I

Of that terrible landscape,
Such as no mortal ever saw,
This morning the image,
Vague and distant, still excites me.

Sleep is full of miracles!
By a strange caprice
I had banished from that spectacle
Irregular vegetation,

And, a painter proud of my talent,
I enjoyed in my picture
The intoxicating monotony
Of metal, marble and water.

Babel of stairways and arcades,
It was an endless palace,
Full of reservoirs and cascades
Falling into a dull or darkened gold;

And heavy cataracts,
Like crystal curtains,
Hung, in shimmering light,
On metal walls.

Not with trees, but with colonnades
The sleeping ponds were surrounded,
Where huge nymphs,
Like women, were mirrored.

Sheets of water spread out, blue,
Between rose and green quays,
Through millions of leagues,
Toward the ends of the universe;

They were unheard-of stones
And magic waves; they were

Huge dazzling glaciers
In all they reflected!

Carefree and taciturn,
Ganges Rivers, in the firmament,
Poured the treasure of their urns
Into diamond abysses.

Architect of my own fantasies,
I made pass, at will,
Under a tunnel of precious stones
A conquered ocean;

And everything, even the color black,
Seemed polished, clear, prismatic;
The liquid encased its glory
In the crystallized ray.

There was no star, no vestige
Of a sun, even at the horizon of the sky,
To illumine these prodigies,
Which shone with a personal fire!

And over these moving marvels
Hovered (a terrifying novelty!
Everything for the eye, nothing for the ear!)
A silence of eternity.

II

On opening again my eyes full of flame
I saw the horror of my garret,
And felt, as I turned inwardly,
The sharp prick of accursed worries;

The clock with the funereal tones
Struck noon brutally,
And the sky poured darkness
Over the sad lethargic world.

The Morning Twilight

Reveille sounded in the courtyard of the barracks,
And the morning wind blew on the lanterns.

It was the hour when the swarm of guilty dreams
Twists dark-haired adolescents on their pillows;
When, like a bleeding eye which throbs and moves,
The lamp makes a red spot on the daylight;
When the soul, under the weight of a reluctant heavy body,
Imitates the struggle between the lamp and the daylight.
Like a face covered with tears which the wind dries,
The air is full of the shuddering of things which flee,
And man is tired of writing and woman of loving.

Houses here and there began to send up smoke.
Prostitutes, with white eyelids,
And opened mouths, slept their stupid sleep;
Impoverished women, dragging their thin old breasts,
Blew on their burning logs and blew on their fingers.
It was the hour when in the cold and stinginess
The pain of women in labor grows greater;
Like a sob interrupted by thick blood
The distant song of the cock ripped through the foggy air;
A sea of fogs bathed the buildings,
And the dying in the depths of the hospitals
Uttered their last rattle in uneven gasps.
The revelers went home, broken by their work.

Shivering dawn in a rose-and-green dress
Slowly advanced over the deserted Seine,
And dark Paris, rubbing his eyes,
Took hold of his tools, a hard-working old man.

Destruction

Ceaselessly beside me the Demon writhes;
He swarms around me like impalpable air;
I swallow him and feel him burning my lungs
And filling them with an everlasting guilty desire.

At times he takes, knowing my great love for Art,
The form of the most seductive of women,
And, under specious pretexts of depression,
Accustoms my lips to infamous love charms.

Thus, far from the sight of God, he leads me,
Panting and crushed by fatigue, into the midst
Of the plains of Boredom, extensive and deserted,

And throws before my eyes full of confusion
Soiled clothing, opened wounds,
And the bloody apparatus of Destruction.

A Martyr

Drawing of an Unknown Master

In the midst of flasks, gilt fabrics
    And rich furniture,
Marbles, pictures perfumed dresses,
    Dragging with sumptuous folds,

In a warm room where, as in a hothouse,
    The air is dangerous and fatal,
Where dying bouquets in their glass caskets
    Exhale their last sigh,

A headless corpse sends forth, like a river,
    On the slaked pillow
A red living blood, which the cloth soaks up
    With the avidity of a meadow.

Similar to the pale visions which the darkness engenders
    And which captivate our eyes,
The head, with the mass of its dark hair
    And its precious jewels,

On the night table, like a ranunculus,
    Rests; and, emptied of thoughts,
A glance vague and white as twilight,
    Escapes from the revulsed eyes.

On the bed, the naked torso displays without scruple
    In the completest abandonment
The secret splendor and the fatal beauty
    With which nature endowed it;

On the leg, a rose-colored stocking, decorated with gold clocks,
    Remains like a souvenir;
The garter, like a flaming secret eye,
    Darts a diamondlike glance.

The singular aspect of this solitude
    And of a large languorous portrait,
With eyes as provocative as its pose,
    Reveals a secretive love,

A guilty joy and strange orgies
    Full of infernal kisses,
Over which the swarm of bad angels rejoiced
    As they swarm in the folds of the curtains;

And yet, on seeing the elegant thinness
    Of the shoulder with its abrupt shape,
The hip a bit pointed and the frisky figure
    Like an irritated snake,

She is still quite young! Had her exasperated soul
    And her senses bitten by boredom
Half opened to the greedy pack
    Of errant lost desires?

Did the vindictive man you were not able, when alive,
    In spite of so much love, to satisfy,
Release over your inert and complacent flesh
    The immensity of his desire?

Answer, impure corpse! And through your stiff tresses,
    Raising you with a feverish arm,
Tell me, terrifying head, did he on your cold teeth
    Imprint the last farewell?

—Far from the mocking world, far from the impure crowd,
    Far from curious magistrates,
Sleep in peace, sleep in peace, strange creature,
    In your mysterious tomb;

Your lover is far away, and your immortal form
    Watches near him when he sleeps;
As much as you doubtless he will be faithful
    And constant until death.

A Voyage to Cythera

My heart, like a bird, flew about joyously
And hovered in freedom around the riggings;
The ship rolled under a sky without clouds,
Like an angel intoxicated with a radiant sun.

What is this sad dark island? It is Cythera,
They tell us, a famous country in songs,
The banal Eldorado of all the playboys.
Look! After all, it's a poor land.

—Island of sweet secrets and celebrations of the heart!
The proud phantom of ancient Venus
Hovers above your seas like an aroma,
And fills the mind with love and languor.

Beautiful island with green myrtle, full of opened flowers,
Venerated forever by all nations,
Where the sigh of adoring hearts
Rolls like incense over a garden of roses

Or the eternal cooing of a turtledove!
—Cythera was but a land of the most wasted kind,
A rocky desert disturbed by bitter cries.
Yet I cold half distinguish an unusual object!

It was not a temple with bosky shadows,
Where the young priestess, lover of flowers,
Walked, her body burning with secret fire,
And her dress half opening in the passing breeze;

But there as we gazed the coast close enough
To disturb the birds with our white sails,
We saw it was a three-forked gallows,
Standing out in black from the sky, like a cypress.

Ravenous birds perched on their prey
Were ferociously demolishing a ripe body that had been hanged,
Each one planting, like an instrument, its impure beak
In all the bleeding parts of the rotting flesh;

The eyes were two holes, and from the collapsed belly
The heavy intestines flowed over the thighs,
And its tormentors, gorged with hideous food,
Had totally castrated it with their sharp beaks.

Under its feet, a flock of jealous beasts,
With uplifted muzzles, were moving and prowling about;
A very large animal in the middle behaved
Like a leader surrounded by his aides.

Inhabitant of Cythera, child of so beautiful a sky,
In silence you bore these insults
As expiation for your infamous cults
And for the sins which deprived you of a tomb.

Ridiculous victim of the gallows, your grief is mine!
When I saw your floating limbs, I felt,
Mounting toward my mouth, like a vomiting
The long stream of bile of old grief;

Before you, poor wretch with so precious a memory,
I felt all the beaks and all the jaws
Of lancinating crows and black panthers
Who once dearly loved to tear my flesh.

—The sky was charming, the sea unclouded;
For me all would be henceforth black and bloody,
Alas! and I had, as in a thick shroud,
Buried my heart in this allegory.

In your island, O Venus, I found standing
Only a symbolic gallows from which my image was hanging . . .
—O Lord, give me the strength and the courage
To contemplate without disgust my heart and my body!

Death of the Lovers

We shall have beds full of faint perfumes,
Divans as deep as tombs,
And strange flowers on shelves,
Opened for us under more beautiful skies.

Using their last warmth in emulation,
Our two hearts will be two vast torches,
Which will reflect their double lights
In our two spirits, those twin mirrors.

One evening, made of mystical rose and blue,
We will exchange one flash of light,
Like a long sob, laden with farewells;

And later an Angel, half opening the doors,
Will come, faithful and joyous, to reanimate
The tarnished mirrors and the dead flames.

Death of the Artists

How many times must I shake my clown's bells
And kiss your low brow, sad caricature?
In order to strike the target, of mystical nature,
How many javelins must I lose, O quiver?

We will wear out our souls in subtle schemes,
And dismantle many a heavy armor,
Before contemplating the great Creature
Whose infernal desire fills us with sobs!

There are some who have never known their Idol,
And those banned sculptors branded with an affront,
Who as they walk beat their chests and their brows,

Have but one hope, strange and somber Capitol!
It is that Death, hovering like a new sun,
Will cause the flowers of their minds to bloom!

The Voyage

To Maxime Du Camp

I

For the child, in love with maps and prints,
The universe is equal to his huge appetite.
Ah! how large the world is under the lamplight!
In the eyes of memory, how small the world is!

One morning we leave, our minds full of fire,
Our hearts heavy with anger and bitter desire,
And we go, following the rhythm of the wave,
Rocking our infinity on the finiteness of the sea:

Some, happy to escape from an infamous land;
Others, from the horror of their cradles, and a few,
Astrologists drowning in the eyes of a woman,
A tyrannical Circe with her dangerous perfumes.

In order not to be changed into beasts, they are enraptured
With space and light and burning skies;
The ice which freezes them, the sun which bronzes them,
Slowly efface the mark of kisses.

But the real travelers are those only who leave
In order to leave; light hearts, similar to balloons,
They are never separated from their fate,
And, without knowing why, always say: let us go on!

Those whose desires have the form of clouds,
And who dream, as a recruit dreams of a cannon,
Of vast, changing, and unknown raptures,
And whose name the human spirit has never known!

II

We imitate, O horror, the top and the bowl
In their waltz and their leap; even in our sleep
Curiosity torments and rolls us,
As a cruel Angel whipping the sun.

Singular fortune where the goal is displaced,
And, being nowhere, can be anywhere!
Where Man, whose hope never wearies,
In order to find rest is always rushing like a fool!

Our soul is a three-master searching for its Icaria;
A voice resounds on the deck: "Open your eyes!"
A voice from the watch, ardent and mad, cries:
"Love . . . fame . . . happiness!" Hell! it is a reef!

Each island pointed out by the watchman
Is an Eldorado promised by Destiny;
The Imagination which calls up its orgy
Finds only a sandbar in the morning light.

O the poor lover of chimerical lands!
Shall we put into irons, and cast into the sea,
This drunken sailor, inventor of Americas
Whose mirage makes the deep more bitter?

As the old tramp, groveling in the mud,
Dreams, his nose in the air, of brilliant paradises;
His bewitched eyes discover a Capua
Wherever the candle lights up a hovel.

III

Amazing travelers! What noble histories
We read in your eyes as deep as the sea!
Show us the caskets of your rich memories,
The marvelous jewels, made of stars and rays.

We want to voyage without steam and without sail!
To enliven the boredom of our prisons,
Send over our minds, as taut as a canvas,
Your memories with their frames of horizons.

Tell me, what did you see?

IV

"We saw stars
And waves; we saw sand also;

And, despite many shocks and unforeseen disasters,
We were often bored, as here.

The glory of the sun on the violet sea,
The glory of the cities in the setting sun,
Lighted up in our hearts a restless yearning
To plunge into a sky with an alluring reflection.

The richest cities, the widest landscapes,
Never contained the mysterious attraction
Of those which chance creates with clouds.
And always desire made us worried!

—Satisfaction adds strength to desire.
Desire, old tree to which pleasure serves as manure,
While your bark grows and hardens,
Your branches want to see the sun at closer range!

Will you continue to grow, huge tree with longer life
Than the cypress?—But we have carefully
Picked a few sketches for your voracious album,
Brothers who find beautiful everything that comes from far off!

We have greeted idols with a trunk;
Thrones studded with luminous jewels;
Decorated palaces whose fantasylike pomp
Would be for your bankers a ruinous dream;

Costumes which are an intoxication for the eyes:
Women whose teeth and nails are tinted,
And learned jugglers caressed by a serpent."

V

And after that, what after that?

VI

"O childish minds!

In order not to forget the important thing,
We have seen everywhere, and without looking for it,

From the top to the bottom of the fatal ladder,
The boring spectacle of immortal sin:

Woman, a low slave, proud and stupid,
Worshiping herself without laughter and loving herself without disgust;
Man, a greedy tyrant, lustful, hard and envious,
Slave of the slave and rivulet in the sewer;

The executioner who has his pleasure, the martyr who sobs;
The festivity heightened and perfumed by blood;
The poison of power irritating the despot,
And the crowd in love with the crushing whip;

Several religions similar to ours,
All of them climbing to heaven; His Holiness,
As on a feather bed a refined man wallows,
In nails and horeshair looking for his pleasure;

Talkative Humanity, intoxicated on its genius,
And, mad now as it once was,
Crying to God, in its crazed agony:
"O man like myself, O master, I curse you!"

And the least foolish, bold lovers of Madness,
Fleeing the large flock impounded by Destiny,
And taking refuge in the immensity of opium
—Such is the eternal record of the entire globe."

VII

It is bitter knowledge one derives from travel!
The world, monotonous and small, today,
Yesterday, tomorrow, always, shows us our own image:
An oasis of horror in a desert of boredom!

Should we leave? or stay? If you can stay, stay;
Leave, if you must. One man runs, and the next hides
To trick the vigilant fatal enemy,
Time! There are, alas, continual runners,

Like the wandering Jew and like the apostles,

To whom nothing suffices, neither train nor ship,
In order to flee the infamous retiary; there are others
Who can kill him without leaving their cradle.

When at last he puts his foot on our neck,
We can hope and shout: Forward!
As once we left for China,
Our eyes fixed seaward and our hair in the wind,

We shall embark on the sea of darkness
With the joyous heart of a young passenger.
Do you hear those voices, charming and funereal,
Singing: "Come this way, you who wish to eat

The perfumed Lotus! this is where men harvest
The miraculous fruits your heart hungers for;
Come and intoxicate yourself on the strange sweetness
Of that afternoon which never ends"?

By his familiar accent we sense the ghost;
Our Pylades over there extend their arms to us.
"To refresh your courage, swim toward your Electra!"
Says the girl whose knees we once kissed.

VIII

O Death, old captain, the time has come! Let us weigh anchor!
This land bores us, O Death! Let us set sail!
If the sky and the sea are as black as ink,
Our hearts which you know are filled with rays!

Pour your poison so that it will comfort us!
The fire searing our brain is such that we want
To plunge to the bottom of the abyss, whether it be Heaven or
Hell,
To the bottom of the Unknown in order to find something *new*!

Lesbos

Mother of Roman games and Greek pleasures,
Lesbos, where kisses, languid or joyous,
Warm as the sun, cool as watermelons,
Are the ornament of nights and glorious days;
Mother of Roman games and Greek pleasures,

Lesbos, where kisses are like cascades
Which fall fearlessly into bottomless gulfs,
And hasten, sobbing and slipping by jerks,
Stormy and secretive, swarming and deep;
Lesbos, where kisses are like cascades!

Lesbos, where Phrynes attract one another,
Where a sigh never remained without an echo,
On a par with Paphos the stars admire you,
And Venus can rightfully be jealous of Sappho!
Lesbos, where Phrynes attract one another,

Lesbos, land of warm and languorous nights,
Which force, O sterile ardor, before their mirrors,
Girls with hollow eyes and amorous bodies
To caress the ripe fruits of their puberty;
Lesbos, land of warm and languorous nights,

Let the severe eyes of old Plato frown;
You exact your pardon from the excess of kisses,
Queen of the sweet empire, loving and noble land,
And of the always inexhaustible subtleties.
Let the severe eyes of old Plato frown.

You exact your pardon from the eternal pain,
Inflicted without respite on ambitious hearts,
Attracted far from us by the radiant smile
Vaguely perceived at the edge of other skies!
You exact your pardon from the eternal pain!

Lesbos, which of the gods will dare be your judge
And condemn your brow grown pale by your work,
If his golden scales have not weighed the deluge
Of tears which your weeping has poured into the sea?
Lesbos, which of the gods will dare be your judge?

What do the laws of the just and the unjust demand of us?
Virgins with noble hearts, honor of the isles,
Your religion like others is solemn,
And love will laugh at Hell and Heaven!
What do the laws of the just and the unjust demand of us?

For Lesbos has chosen me among all men of the earth
To sing the secret of its flowering virgins,
And as a child I was admitted to the dark mystery
Of frantic laughter mingled with somber tears;
For Lesbos has chosen me among all men of the earth.

From then on I have watched at the top of Leucate,
Like a sentinel with a piercing and accurate eye,
Who watches day and night for brig, tartan or frigate,
Whose distant shapes quiver in the blue;
From then on I have watched at the top of Leucate,

To know whether the sea is indulgent and kind,
And in the sobs with which the rock resounds
One evening will bring back to Lesbos, which forgives,
The worshiped body of Sappho, who left,
To know whether the sea is indulgent and kind!

Of mannish Sappho, lover and poet
More beautiful than Venus in her sad pallor!
—The blue eye is vanquished by the black eye spotted
By the dark circle traced by the suffering
Of mannish Sappho, lover and poet!

—More beautiful than Venus rising over the world
And pouring forth the abundance of her calm
And the radiance of her blond youthfulness
Over the old Ocean delighted with his daughter;
More beautiful than Venus rising over the world!

—Of Sappho who died on the day of her blasphemy,
When, insulting the rite and the designated worship,
She made her beautiful body the supreme prey
Of a brute whose pride punished the impiety
Of the one who died on the day of her blasphemy.

And it is since that time that Lesbos laments,
And, despite the honors which the world pays it,
Exalts every night with the cry of the torment
Which its deserted banks raise toward heaven!
And it is since that time that Lesbos laments!

The Fountain

Your beautiful eyes are tired, beloved!
Stay for a long time, without opening them,
In that relaxed pose
Where pleasure left you.
In the courtyard the chattering fountain
Which does not stop night or day,
Sweetly sustains the ecstasy
Into which love this evening plunged me.

> The sheaf opening
>   Into a thousand flowers,
> Where the joyous moon
>   Places its colors,
> Falls like a rain
>   Of heavy tears.

Thus your soul enflamed
By the burning light of pleasure
Rushes, swift and bold,
Toward the vast enchanted skies.
Then, it spills forth, dying,
In a wave of sad languor,
Which along an invisible slope
Descends to the bottom of my heart.

> The sheaf opening
>   Into a thousand flowers,
> Where the joyous moon
>   Places its colors,
> Falls like a rain
>   Of heavy tears.

Beloved, whom the night makes beautiful,
How I love, as I bend over your heart,
To listen to the eternal lament
Which sobs in the fountains!
Moon, sonorous water, blessed night,
Trees trembling nearby,
Your pure melancholy
Is the mirror of my love.

The sheaf opening
Into a thousand flowers,
Where the joyous moon
Places its colors,
Falls like a rain
Of heavy tears.

To a Malabar Girl

Your feet are as refined as your hands, and your hip
Is wide enough to cause envy in the whitest hip;
To the pensive artist your body is sweet and dear;
Your large velvet eyes are blacker than your skin.
In the warm blue country where God had you born,
Your duty is to light the pipe of your master.

To provide the flasks of cold water and perfumes,
To keep far from the bed all curious mosquitoes,
And, as soon as the morning brings a song to the plane trees,
To buy pineapples and bananas at the bazaar.
All day, wherever you wish, you walk with bare feet,
And softly hum old unknown melodies;
And when evening in its scarlet mantle falls,
You gently stretch your body on a mat,
Where your floating dreams are full of hummingbirds,
And always, like yourself, peaceful and flowering.

Why, happy child, do you want to see our France,
An overpopulated country which suffering mows down,
And, entrusting your life to the strong arms of sailors,
Say grand farewells to your beloved tamarinds?
Half-clothed as you are, with thin muslin,
Shivering in France under snow and hail,
How you would weep for your sweet carefree leisure,
If, with a brutal corset imprisoning your flanks,
You had to glean your supper in our mud
And sell the perfume of your strange charms,
Your eyes pensive, and watching, in our filthy fog,
The scattered phantoms of absent cocoa palms!

Epigraph for a Condemned Book

Peaceful bucolic reader,
Sober naïve man of good will,
Throw away this saturnine
Orgiastic and melancholy book.

Unless you have studied your rhetoric
With Satan, that wily dean,
Throw it away! You would not understand it,
Or you would believe my hysterical.

But if, without allowing them to be spellbound,
Your eyes can see into abysses,
Read me, in order to learn to love me;

Curious soul who suffer
And are looking for your paradise,
Pity me! . . . Otherwise, I curse you!

Meditation

Behave, O my Grief, and keep still.
You asked for Evening; it is descending; here it is:
A dark atmosphere covers the city,
Bearing peace to some, and worry to others.

While the wretched crowd of mortals,
Under the whip of Pleasure, that merciless torturer,
Goes to collect remorse in the servile festivity,
My Grief, give me your hand; come this way,

Far off from them. See the Years that have died leaning
Over the balconies of heaven, in old-fashioned dresses;
See my Regret in smiles rising up from the depths of the water;

The dying Sun going to sleep under an arch,
And, like a long shroud dragging toward the East,
Hear, my beloved, hear the steps of sweet night.

The Abyss

Pascal had his abyss, which moved with him.
Alas! everything is an abyss—action, desire, dreams,
Words! and over my hair which stands upright
I often feel the wind of Fear pass.

Above and below, everywhere, distances, shores,
Silence, terrifying imprisoning space . . .
Over the depths of my nights God with His knowing finger
Draws a multiform traceless nightmare.

I fear sleep as one fears a great hole,
Full of vague horror, leading one knows not where;
I see only infinity through all my windows,

And my mind, always haunted by vertigo,
Is jealous of the insensibility of the void.
—Ah! I will never be free of Numbers and Beings!

Complaints of an Icarus

The lovers of prostitutes
Are happy, free and satisfied;
As for me, my arms are broken
Over embracing clouds.

Thanks to the extraordinary stars,
Which shine in the depths of the sky,
My consumed eyes see only
Memories of suns.

In vain I tried to find
The end of space and its middle;
Under some fiery eye or other
I feel my wing breaking;

And burned by love of beauty,
I will not have the sublime honor
Of giving my name to the abyss
Which will serve me as a tomb.

PARIS SPLEEN

PARIS SELLER

The Stranger

Whom do you prefer, enigmatical man, tell me, your father, your mother, your sister or your brother?

I have no father, nor mother, nor sister, nor brother.

Your friends?

There you're using a word whose meaning has remained thus far unknown to me.

Your country?

I do not know under what latitude it is situated.

Beauty?

Willingly would I love her, goddess and immortal.

Gold?

I hate it as you hate God.

So, what do you love, unusual stranger?

I love clouds . . . the clouds which pass by . . . over yonder . . . over yonder . . . the marvelous clouds!

The Artist's *Confiteor*

How piercing are the endings of autumn days! Piercing until they bring on pain! For there are certain exciting sensations whose vagueness does not exclude intensity; and there is no sharper point than that of Infinity.

What a delight it is to look deeply into the immensity of the sky and the sea! Solitude, silence, incomparable chastity of blue! A small sail trembling on the horizon, which in its smallness and isolation imitates my irremediable life, the monotonous melody of the surge, all of these things think through me, or I think through them (for in the greatness of dreams, the *ego* is quickly lost!); they think, I repeat, but musically and in a picturesque way, without quibbling, without syllogisms and without deductions.

However, these thoughts, whether they come from me or rush forth from things, soon become too intense. Vigor in pleasure created discomfort and a decided suffering. My overtaut nerves give our noisy and painful vibrations.

And now the depths of the sky terrify me; its clearness exasperates me. The insensibility of the sea and the immortality of its spectacle disgust me. . . . Ah! must I always suffer, or always avoid beauty? Abandon me, nature, sorceress without mercy, ever triumphant rival! Stop tempting my desires and my pride! The study of beauty is a duel in which the artist cries out from fear before he is conquered.

The Double Room

A room which resembles a dream, a truly *spiritual* room, in which an atmosphere of stagnation is slightly tinted with rose and blue.

There the soul takes a bath of idleness, with the pungent odors of regret and desire. It is something crepuscular, bluish and rosy; a dream of pleasure during an eclipse.

The furniture has elongated, prostrated and languishing forms. The furniture seems to be dreaming. You might say it is endowed with a somnambulist life, like the vegetable and the mineral. The fabrics speak a mute language, like flowers, skies, and setting suns.

On the walls there is no artistic abomination. In its relationship to a pure dream, to an unanalyzed impression, definite art, positive art is blasphemy. Here, everything has a sufficient light and the charming darkness of harmony.

An infinitesimal odor of the most exquisite choice, to which is joined a very slight humidity, floats in this atmosphere, where the slumbering spirit is rocked by sensations of a greenhouse.

Muslin falls abundantly in front of the windows and the bed; it drops in snowy cascades. On the bed is lying the Idol, the goddess of dreams. But how is she here? Who has brought her? What magic power placed her on this throne of dreams and pleasure? What difference does it make? She is here and I recognize her.

Yes, these are her eyes whose fire cuts through the evening light; her subtle terrible *eyes* I recognize by their fearful malice! They attract, and subjugate, and devour, the glance of the man imprudent enough to look upon them. I have often studied those black stars which command our curiosity and admiration.

What kindly demon has seen to it that I am thus surrounded by mystery, silence, peace and perfumes? O beatitude! What we generally call life, even in its happiest expansion, has nothing in common which this supreme life I now know and savor minute by minute, second by second!

No! There are no more minutes and no more seconds! Time has disappeared; eternity now reigns, an eternity of pleasure!

But a fearful, heavy blow resounded against the door, and, as in my dreams of hell, I seemed to receive the blow of a pickaxe in my stomach.

And then a Ghost came in. A bailiff coming to torment me in the name of the law; an infamous concubine coming to cry poverty and add the trivialities of her life to sufferings of mine; or the errand boy of a newspaper director asking for the rest of a manuscript.

The heavenly room, the idol, the dream goddess, the *Sylphide*, as great René used to say, all that magic vanished with the brutal knock struck by the Ghost.

O horror! I remember! I remember! Yes! That hovel, that place of eternal boredom is mine. Here is the stupid dusty worn-out furniture: the hearthside with no flame and no embers, filthy with spittle; the gloomy windows where rain traced streaks in the dust; the manuscripts scratched out or incomplete; the almanac where a pencil had marked the ominous dates!

And that perfume of another world, on which with perfected sensibility I had gotten drunk, alas, was replaced by a tobacco stench mingled with a nauseating moldiness. Now we breathe here the rancidness of desolation.

In this narrow world, which is so full of disgust, a single known object smiles at me: the vial of laudanum; an old and fearful friend; and like all friends, alas, fertile in caresses and betrayals.

Oh, yes! Time has reappeared; time reigns as a sovereign now, and with the hideous old man has come back all of his demoniacal procession of Memories, Regrets, Spasms, Fear, Anxieties, Nightmares, Anger and Neuroses.

I assure you that now the seconds are strongly and solemnly accented, and each one, as it gushes forth from the clock, says: "I am Life, unbearable, implacable Life!"

There is only one Second in a human life which has the mission of announcing *good news*, the good news which creates in each one an inexplicable fear.

Yes! Times reigns; it has recovered its brutal dictatorship. And it pushes on, with its double goad, as if I were an ox. "Go on, she-ass! Sweat, slave! Live, soul in hell!"

Each of Us Has His Chimera

Under a wide gray sky, in a big dusty plain, without roads, or grass, or thistle, or nettle, I met several men who were walking bent over.

Each of them carried on his back a huge Chimera, as heavy as a bag of flour or coal, or the equipment of a Roman foot soldier.

But the monstrous beast was not an inert weight; on the contrary, it covered and oppressed the man with its elastic, powerful muscles; it fastened itself with its two large claws on the chest of its mount; and its fabulous head rose above the man's head, like one of those horrible helmets by which ancient warriors hoped to instill terror in the enemy.

I questioned one of those men, and asked him where they were going in this way. He answered that neither he nor the others knew anything about it; but that obviously they were going somewhere, since they were impelled by an invincible need to walk.

One curious thing to note: no one of these travelers seemed irritated with the wild beast hanging on his neck and glued to his back; you might say he looked upon it as part of himself. All those weary serious-looking faces gave no evidence of despair; under the mournful cupola of the sky, where their feet sank into the dust of an earth as sad as the sky, they walked on with the resigned faces of those who are eternally condemned to hope.

And the procession passed beside me and disappeared into the atmosphere on the horizon, at the spot where the rounded surface of the planet withdraws from the curiosity of human eyes.

And for a few seconds I persisted in trying to understand this mystery; but soon irresistible Indifference closed over me, and I was more heavily crushed by it than they themselves were by their weighty Chimeras.

The Wicked Maker of Window Glass

There are purely contemplative natures quite unsuitable for action, which however, under a mysterious and unknown impulse, at times act with a swiftness of which they themselves would have felt incapable.

Like the man who, afraid of being given bad news by his concierge, cravenly walks back and forth an hour in front of his door without daring to go in, or like the man who keeps a letter for two weeks without opening it, or like the man who after six months undertakes to perform a duty which had been necessary to do for a year—at times these men feel abruptly precipitated into action by an irresistible force, like an arrow from a bow. The moralist and the doctor, who imagine they know everything, cannot explain whence comes so suddenly so wild an energy in these lazy pleasure-seeking souls and how they, incapable of accomplishing the most simple and the most necessary things, find at a certain moment the abundant courage to carry out the most absurd and often the most dangerous acts.

One of my friends, the most inoffensive dreamer who ever existed, once set fire to a forest in order to see, he said, whether fire would catch on as easily as is generally believed. Ten successive times, the experiment failed; but on the eleventh, it succeeded far too well.

Someone else will light a cigar near a powder barrel, *to see, to know, to tempt fate*, to force himself to prove his energy, to play the gambler, to know the pleasure of anxiety, or for no reason, through caprice, because of idleness.

It is a kind of energy rising out of boredom and dreams; and those in whom it is so clearly manifested are, in general, as I have said, the most indolent and the most pensive of all.

Another, shy to the point of lowering his eyes even before the eyes of other men, to the point of having to muster all his poor will power in order to enter a café or pass in front of the box office of a theater, where the ticket collectors seem to him to be vested with the majesty of Minos, Eacus and Rhadamanthus, will unexpectedly rush up to an old man passing near him and embrace him fervently to the amazement of all present.

Why? Was it because . . . because he was strongly attracted to that man's face? Perhaps; but it is safer to suppose that he himself does not know why.

More than once I have been a victim of those crises and impulses, which entitle us to believe that malicious Demons slyly enter us and force us to carry out, without our knowing it, their most absurd manifestations of will.

One morning I had gotten up sullen, sad, weary, with idleness, and impelled, as it seemed to me, to do something big, a startling deed; and I opened the window, alas!

(I beg you to observe that the spirit of mystification which, with some, is not the result of work or contrivance, but of fortuitous inspiration, largely shares—even if it is merely in the ardor of desire—in that disposition, hysterical according to physicians, satanic according to those who think more clearly than physicians, which impels us without our resisting toward many dangerous or indecorous actions.)

The first person I saw in the street was a maker of window-glass whose piercing, dissonant cry mounted through the heavy dank Paris air to where I was. It would be impossible for me to say why with regard to that poor fellow such a sudden and despotic hate seized me.

"Hey, hey!" And I shouted to him to come up. In the meantime I thought, not without some delight, that the room, being on the seventh floor and the stairway very narrow, the man would have trouble in completing his ascent and would catch in many places the corners of his fragile merchandise.

At last he appeared; with curiosity I examined all of his window panes, and said to him: "What! You don't have any colored glass? No rose, red, blue window panes? No magic panes? No paradise panes? What impudence! You dare walk about in poor neighborhoods, and you don't even have any glass which will show how beautiful life is!" And I pushed him briskly toward the stairway, where he stumbled and groaned.

I went to the balcony and took up a small pot of flowers, and when the man reappeared at the door exit, I dropped my war machine perpendicularly on the back edge of his brackets; the impact toppled him, and under his back he shattered all of his poor ambulatory fortune which made the sharp noise of a crystal palace struck by lightning.

Drunk with madness, I shouted furiously at him: "How beautiful life is! How beautiful life is!"

These nervous jokes are not without peril, and you can often pay dearly for them. But of what consequence is the eternity of damnation for the man who found in a second the infinity of pleasure?

Crowds

It is not given to every man to bathe in a multitude: to enjoy a crowd is an art; and only that man is able, at the expense of humanity, to experience a bout of vitality, into whom a fairy has breathed, when he was in his cradle, the taste for travesty and masks, the hate for family life and the passion for traveling.

Multitude, solitude: synonymous terms and convertible by the active and creative poet. He who cannot people his solitude, cannot be alone in a busy crowd.

The poet enjoys the incomparable privilege of being at will himself and someone else. Like those wandering souls looking for a body, he enters, when he wishes to, the personality of each man. For him alone, everything is opened; if certain places seem closed to him, that is because for him they are not worth the trouble of being visited.

The solitary meditative walker draws an unusual excitement from this universal communion. The man who easily joins with the crowd knows feverish pleasures, of which the egotist, closed like a chest, and the lazy person, imprisoned like a mollusc, will forever be deprived. He adopts all professions as his own, all the joys and woes which circumstance presents to him.

What men call love is very small, limited and weak, compared with that ineffable orgy, that holy prostitution of the soul which gives itself completely, poetry and charity, to the unforeseen which appears, to the unknown which passes by.

It is good sometimes to tell the lucky ones in this world, even if it is only to humiliate for a moment their foolish pride, that there is a happiness superior to theirs, vaster and more refined. Founders of colonies, pastors of people, missionary priests exiled at the ends of the earth, doubtless know something of this mysterious excitement; and, at the heart of the vast family which their genius has created, they must sometimes laugh at those who pity them for their perturbed fortune and their chaste life.

The Old Clown

The people on vacation sprawled everywhere, spread out, and rollicked. It was one of the feast days on which, long in advance, clowns, mountebanks, animal trainers and peddlers rely to make up for the bad seasons of the year.

On those days it seems to me the people forget everything, suffering and work, and behave like children. For the young it is a holiday, the horror of school dismissed for twenty-four hours. For adults it is an armistice signed with the malevolent powers of life, a respite in universal disputes and struggles.

Even the man of the world and the man occupied with spiritual labors do not easily escape the influence of this popular festivity. Without wishing to, they absorb their part of the carefree atmosphere. As for me, in my role of true Parisian, I never fail to inspect all the booths which are proudly displayed at those solemn times.

They were, in truth, carrying on a formidable rivalry: squealing, bellowing, and shouting. It was a mingling of cries, and detonations from the brass and rocket explosions. The red-tailed devils and the fools twisted the features of their faces, tanned and toughened by wind, rain and sun. With the self-possession of actors sure of their effect, they yelled out witticisms and jokes of a solid heavy humor, like Molière's. The muscle men, proud of the size of their limbs, without brow or cranium, resembling orang-outangs, appeared majestic and solemn dressed in their tights which had been washed the day before the occasion. Dancers, as beautiful as fairies or princesses, jumped and capered in the flame of lanterns which made their skirts sparkle.

It was all light, dust, cries, happiness, uproar; some were spending money, and others earning it, but all were equally joyful. Children were pulling on the skirts of their mothers to get a stick of candy, or climbing up on the shoulders of their fathers to have a better view of a magician as dazzling as a god. And everywhere, dominating all perfumes, there spread a smell of frying which was the incense for this feast.

At the end, at the extreme end of the row of booths—as if, in shame, he had exiled himself from all this splendor—I saw a poor clown, bent over, frail, decrepit, a man ruined, leaning with his back against one of the poles of his hut; this hut was more wretched than that of the lowest savage, its poverty lit up by two ends of candles that were melting and smoking.

Everywhere joy, profit and dissoluteness; everywhere the assurance of bread for tomorrow; everywhere the frenzied explosion of vigor. But here absolute poverty, poverty bedecked, as a crowning horror, with comic rags, where need, much more than art, had introduced contrast. The wretch did not laugh! He did not weep or dance or gesticulate or shout; he sang neither a gay nor a sad song, he did not supplicate. He was mute and motionless. He had given up, he had abdicated. His destiny was over.

But he was looking in a deep unforgettable way at the crowd and the lights, whose moving mass stopped a few paces off from his repulsive dereliction! I felt my throat tighten under the terrible hand of hysteria, and it seemed to me that my eyes were clouded by those rebellious tears which will not fall.

What could I do? Was there any point in asking the unfortunate man what curiosity, what marvel he had to show in the stinking darkness, behind his torn curtain? Truth to tell, I did not dare ask; and even if you laugh at the reason for my timidity, I will confess that I feared humiliating him. In short, I had just made up my mind to leave some money on one of his boards as I passed by, hoping he would guess my intention, when a great surge of people, caused by some trouble or other, dragged me far away from him.

As I turned around, obsessed by that vision, I tried to analyze my sudden sorrow, and said to myself: I have just seen the image of the old man of letters who has survived the generation for whom he was the brilliant entertainer; the image of the old poet without friends or family or children, degraded by his poverty and the ingratitude of his public, and standing at the booth which the forgetful world no longer has any desire to enter!

The Poor Boy's Toy

I want to convey the idea of an innocent diversion. There are so few pastimes which are not blameworthy!

When you leave the house in the morning with the firm intention of strolling along the main streets, fill your pockets with those inexpensive small inventions—such as the flat jumping jack manipulated by a single string, blacksmiths striking the anvil, the rider with a horse whose tail is a whistle—and offer them to the neglected and poor children you meet in front of restaurants, where they stand by a tree. You will see their eyes grow immoderately big. At first they won't dare take anything; they won't believe in their good luck. Then their hands will grab the present avidly, and they will run off like cats who go far away from you to eat the piece of food you gave them; these children have learned to distrust man.

On a road, behind the iron gate of a large garden, at the end of which you could see the whiteness of an attractive castle lit up by the sun, there was a beautiful and fresh-complexioned child, dressed in those country clothes which have so much fastidiousness.

Luxury, freedom from care and the habitual display of wealth make those children so charming that you could believe them made from a different substance than the children of an undistinguished or poor class.

Beside him on the grass lay a magnificent toy, as beautiful as its master, varnished, gilded, clothed in a purple robe, and covered with plumes and beads. But the child was paying no attention to his favorite toy, this is what he was looking at:

On the other side of the iron gate, on the road, in the midst of thistles and nettles, there was another child, dirty, frail, sooty, one of those child-waifs whose beauty an impartial eye might discover if, as the eye of a connoisseur guesses the ideal painting under a body varnish, it cleaned the child of the repulsive patina of poverty.

Through the symbolic bars separating two worlds, the main road and the castle, the poor child was showing his own toy to the rich child who was greedily examining it as if it were a rare and strange object. Now, this toy, which the small ragamuffin was irritating by shaking a wire box back and forth, was a live rat! His parents, for economy's sake doubtless, had gotten the toy from life itself.

As the two children laughed fraternally at one another, they showed teeth of a *similar* whiteness.

The Rope

To Edouard Manet

My friend used to say to me, "Illusions are as numerous, perhaps, as relationships among men, or between them and things. And when the illusion disappears, that is to say when we see the being or the fact such as it exists outside of us, we experience a strange feeling, complicated partly by regret for the vanished phantom, partly by a pleasant surprise before the new, before the real fact. If there exists a phenomenon evident, banal, always the same, and of such a nature that no mistake is possible, it is maternal love. It is as difficult to suppose a mother without maternal love as a light without heat; is it not perfectly legitimate, therefore, to attribute to maternal love all the actions and words of a mother which relate to her child? And yet, listen to this little story, in which I was unusually mystified by the most natural illusion.

"My profession of painter impels me to look attentively at faces and facial expressions which I encounter on my way, and you know what pleasure we derive from this faculty which for our eyes makes life more vivid and meaningful than for other men. In the distant neighborhood where I live, and where large spaces covered with grass still separate the buildings, I often noticed a boy whose fiery and mischievous expression appealed to me at first, more than all the others. More than once he modeled for me. At times I made a gypsy out of him, at other times an angel, and still at other times a mythological Cupid. I made him carry the vagabond's violin, the Crown of Thorns and the Nails of the Passion, and the torch of Love. I took such keen pleasure in the comic manner of this boy that one day I begged his parents, who were poor people, to let me have him, and I promised to clothe him well, to give him some money and not to impose on him any other work save that of cleaning my brushes and running my errands. This child, cleaned up, became a charming creature, and the life he led with me seemed to him a paradise, compared to what he would have had to undergo in his father's hovel. Yet I must say that this little fellow amazed me at times by strange fits of precocious sadness, and that he soon showed an immoderate liking for sugar and liqueurs; to such an extent, that one day when I saw he had again committed, in spite of my many warnings, a new theft of this nature, I threatened to send him back to his parents. Then I left, and my business kept me away from home for quite some time.

"Imagine my horror and astonishment when, on entering the house, the first thing I saw was that little fellow, the mischievous companion of my life, hanging from the closet door! His feet almost touched the floor; a chair, which he must have pushed aside with his foot, was over-turned beside him; his head was twisted over one shoulder; his swollen face and his eyes, wide open with a terrifying gaze, made me believe first that he was alive. To get him down was not as easy a job as you may think. He was already stiff, and I had an inexplicable repugnance at the thought of dropping him abruptly to the ground. I had to hold up his entire body with one arm, and with the hand of my other arm, cut the rope. But all was not was over when that was done; the little monster had used a very thin string, which had cut deeply into the flesh, and I had to pry with narrow scissors between the two rings of swollen flesh, in order to release his neck.

"I neglected to tell you that I had called loudly for help; but my neighbors had all refused to come to my aid. In that, they were faithful to the custom of civilized man who—I don't know why—never wants to get mixed up with the business of a hanged man. At last a doctor came and declared that the child had been dead for several hours. Later, when we had to undress him for the burial, the rigidity of the corpse was such that, renouncing hope of bending the limbs, we had to slash and cut his clothes in order to take them off.

"The police inspector, to whom, naturally, I had to report the accident, looked at me quizzically and said: 'There's something fishy about this!' impelled doubtless by some innate desire and habit of frightening, on the off-chance, the innocent as well as the guilty.

"One supreme task remained to be done, and the thought of it alone caused me terrible anguish: I had to inform the parents. My legs refused to take me there. At last I summoned courage. But, to my amazement, the mother showed no emotion, and not a tear trickled from the corner of her eye. I attributed this strange behavior to the horror she must have been feeling, and I remembered the well-known saying, 'The deepest suffering is mute.' As for the father, he merely said, half stupefied, half dreaming: "After all, it is perhaps better that way; he would have come to a bad end anyhow!"

"In the meantime the body lay stretched out on my couch, and, helped by a maid, I was busy with the final details, when the mother came into my studio. She said she wanted to see the body of her son. I could not, in truth, prevent her from enjoying emotionally her grief and refuse this supreme and sad consolation. Then she begged me to show her the place where her child had hanged himself. 'Oh, no, Madame,' I replied, 'that would upset you.' And as my eyes involuntarily turned toward that sinister closet, I saw, with a feeling of disgust mixed with horror and anger, that the nail had remained planted in the panel,

and a long piece of rope was still dangling from it. Quickly I went over
to tear off those last vestiges of the catastrophe, and was about to throw
them out the window, when the poor woman seized my arm and said
to me in an irresistible tone of voice: 'Oh! Monsieur! Give me that, I
beg you, I implore you!' It seemed to me that her despair had doubtless
so bewildered her that now she had feelings of tenderness for what had
served as an instrument of death for her son, and wanted to keep it as
a horrible and precious relic. She seized the nail and the string.

"At last! At last! It was all over! Nothing remained for me to do ex-
cept to resume my work, more avidly than usual, to drive out gradually
that little corpse which haunted the recesses of my mind and whose
ghost wore me out with his wide staring eyes. But the next day I re-
ceived a bundle of letters: some were from tenants of my house, others
from nearby houses; one from the second floor, another from the third,
another from the fourth, and so on; some in a half-joking style, as if
trying to disguise under an obvious banter the sincerity of the request,
others grossly insolent and misspelled, but all concerned with the same
purpose, namely to obtain from me a piece of the fatal and beatific
rope. I must say that among the signers there were more women than
men; but they all, believe me, did not belong to the lowest and com-
monest class. I have kept those letters.

"And then suddenly a light dawned on me, and I understood why
the mother was so bent on snatching the string from me and by what
kind of trade she intended to be consoled."

The Thyrsus

To Franz Liszt

What is a thyrsus? According to the moral and the poetic meaning, it is a sacerdotal emblem in the hands of priests and priestesses celebrating divinity of which they are the interpreters and the servants. But physically it is only a staff, a pure staff, a pole for hops, a vine prop, dry, hard and straight. Around this staff, in its capricious windings, stems and flowers play and frolic, some sinuous and fugitive, and others bent over like bells or reversed cups. And an amazing glory rises up from this complexity of lines and colors, tender or resplendent. It might be said that the curved line and the spiral pay court to the straight line and dance around, in silent worship. Might it not be said that all those delicate corollas, all those calyxes, explosions of perfume and color, dance a mystical fandango around the hieratic staff? And yet, where is the imprudent mortal who dares decide whether the flowers and the vine branches were made for the staff, or whether the staff is only the pretext to show the beauty of the vine branches and the flowers? The thyrsus is the representation of your amazing duality, powerful and venerated master, dear Bacchant of the mysterious and impassioned Beauty. Never did a nymph exasperated by invincible Bacchus shake her thyrsus over the heads of her terrified companions with as much energy and caprice as you wave your genius over the hearts of your brothers. The staff is your will, straight, strong and steady; the flowers are the wandering of your fancy around your will, the feminine element performing around the male her fascinating pirouettes. Straight line and arabesque line, intention and expression, strength of will, sinuosity of the word, unity of the goal, variety of the means, all-powerful and indivisible amalgam of genius, what analyst will have the hateful courage to divide you and separate you?

Dear Liszt, through fog, beyond rivers, above cities where pianos sing your glory, where printing presses translate your wisdom, in whatever place you are, in the beauty of the eternal city or in the fogs of countries of dreamers consoled by Gambrinus, improvising songs of joy and unspeakable grief, or confiding to paper your abstruse meditations, singer of eternal Pleasure and Anguish, philosopher, poet and artist, I greet you in immortality!

Intoxication

You must always be intoxicated. It is the key to all: the one question. In order not to feel the horrible burden of Time breaking your back and bending you toward the earth, you must become drunk, without truce.

But on what? On wine, poetry or virtue, as you wish. But you must get drunk.

And if at times, on the steps of a palace, on the green grass of a ditch, in the mournful solitude of your room, you awaken, and your intoxication is already diminished or gone, ask the wind, the wave, the star, the bird, the clock, everything that flees, everything that groans, everything that rolls, that sings, that speaks, ask what time it is; and the wind, the wave, the star, the bird, the clock will answer you: "It is time to get intoxicated! In order not to be slaves martyred by Time, always become intoxicated! On wine, on poetry or on virtue, as you will."

The Mirror

A frightful man comes in and looks at himself in the mirror.

"Why do you look at yourself in the mirror, since you can't see yourself except with displeasure?"

The frightful man answers me: "Sir, according to the immortal principles of '89, all men are equal in rights; therefore I possess the right to see my image; with pleasure or displeasure, that concerns only my conscience."

In the name of common sense, I was doubtless right; but from the viewpoint of the law, he was not wrong.

The Harbor

A harbor is a delightful resort for a soul tired with life's struggles. The fullness of the sky, the moving architecture of clouds, the changing colors of the sea, the beam from the lighthouses, are a prism marvelously suitable to amuse the eyes without ever tiring them. The slender shapes of the ships, with their complicated rigging, on which the sea swell imprints harmonious oscillations, serve to sustain in the soul the love of rhythm and beauty. And then, especially, there is a kind of mysterious aristocratic pleasure for the man who no longer has any curiosity or ambition, to contemplate, when he is lying in the belvedere or leaning on the pier, all the movements of those leaving and those returning, of those who still have the strength to wish, the desire to travel or grow rich.

Any Where Out of the World

This life is a hospital where each patient is possessed with the desire of changing his bed. One would like to suffer in front of the stove, and another believes he would get well beside the windows.

I have the impression that I would always be comfortable there where I am not, and this question of moving is one I am endlessly discussing with myself.

"Tell me, dear soul, poor chilled soul, what would you think of inhabiting Lisbon? It must be warm there, and you would cheer up like a lizard. That city is on the edge of water; they say it is built of marble, and that its people have such hate of plants that they pull up all the trees. That is a landscape to your taste; a landscape made of light and minerals, and of water to reflect them!"

My soul does not answer.

"Since you like to rest so much, with the spectacle of movement, do you wish to come live in that blissful land, Holland? Perhaps you will find enjoyment in that country whose image you have often admired in museums. What would you think of Rotterdam, you who love forests of masts, and ships moored at the base of houses?"

My soul remains mute.

"Perhaps Batavia would attract you more? There we would find the spirit of Europe married with tropical beauty."

Not a word. Might my soul be dead?

"Have you then reached that point of numbness that you find pleasure in your suffering? If that is the case, let us hasten toward countries which are the analogues of Death. I have found the right thing, poor soul! We will pack our bags for Torneo. Let us go still farther, to the extreme end of the Baltic; farther away still from life, if it is possible; let us settle down at the pole. There the sun grazes the earth only obliquely, and the slow alternations of light and night suppress all variety and increase monotony, the bitter half of the void. There, we can take long baths of darkness, while, for our diversion, the aurora borealis sends us from time to time its rose sheaths, like reflections of fireworks from Hell!"

Finally my soul explodes, and cries out to me in great wisdom: "Any where at all! Provided it is outside of this world!"

Alphabetical List of Titles

Alphabetical List of First Lines